Recolouration
Rough Draft

Jesse Warren

Presentation by *BookLeaf Publishing*

Web: www.bookleafpub.com

E-mail: info@bookleafpub.com

ISBN: 978-93-5744-798-0

First edition 2022

DEDICATION

Thank you for helping me heal, princess.

beneath

cold metal coiled and my lungs cut,
'til dissident dirt and debris,
I was dug from the muck that received blood,
'til the veggies on my plate told me "eat up".

I'll never be better from being buried alive.

worms in the sink

I often feel uncivil.

surrounded by the maggots of the mind,
I'm
wrapped among the carrion,
a knife into the gristle,
filthy as a variant or clean and superficial.
it feels too tough to wash off.
it seems too hard to talk.

10:58 pm

it's a long story.

besides, who parks a limo in their front yard?
you insisted we met him.
nice guy. sleepy and old.
he smiled and said that he rented.

before that, we laid out on black tar,
counting the stars in the heavens.
between those,
we wasted time while the sand was still warm,
and the ant hills weren't on the defensive.

eventually, we decided to head home,
since I had said we'd be back by eleven.

static

sound like the waves,
wade through the days,
all of my minds are too static.
I've taken to numbing my brain,
but I'm scared it's becoming a habit.

camping alone

I woke to the morning mist
gripped 'round my curious feet,
which peeked out beneath sleep
and the comfort of down sheets,
considering clouds that creep
through town corridors soundless,
carefully scouting the day's dawn,
diligent to the dangers of braving the mountains.

out here, the sun rays that broke through
are both breathtaking and countless.
or so I've been told.

stroll past

diatribe spring, rain down from the dark.
she'd spin in circles 'til she grew old,
little did we know it devoured her heart.
saw you through the window like a lost soul,
staring up at the stars.
gentlest laugh while it tore you apart.

you've never been this cold,
before.

just three stops

some days, I'd sink into the moquette seats,
head to the wall, and my bag at my feet.
hold breath briefly as the people pack in,
compressed 'til the tracks creak.

then we'd finally move.

one less playground

that's the thing about this city...
it only exists in my spiralling thoughts.
I could walk along backstreets with no names,
and never get lost.

despite that, I feel lost.
lost and ashamed of the way I react,
ashamed I created this map,
ashamed that I can't seem to find a way back.

I've been told that I author my path,
yet these roads lead nowhere.

a stranger in Italy

we once discussed, at length,
the promise of astrology.
the benefits of confidence
compared to those of modesty.
of taking a risk on the things that you want,
and doing better than you ever
could have possibly thought.

I hope you're still there
with your eyes on the stars.

candles exist

when the power goes out,
there's a little voice in the back of my head
that says: "we're used to the darkness."

it's not reassuring.

12

these streets seem to corrode,
and we spoke in alleys while shivering cold.
ten more blocks just to walk home.
her heartbeat beating beneath
my splintering bones.

this year, she would have been twelve years old.

can't win

what is this paralysis?
associate success with negativity.
mental illness, callousness,
losing faith in my ability.

I'd just like to focus,
I'd just like to breathe.

I'm suffocating underneath these dreams.

a crow aboard

the crow Bijou ceased to beseech,
a timorous speech, seeking the half-truths
beneath a black mass of Kraken-ish teeth,
seized Icarus, a tragedy past due.

a shattering splash crashed brackish and blue,
and there breached, thrashing,
a dragon-ish beast,
fastened to feet and beak seemingly glued,
the crow Bijou ceased to beseech.

unseen from under the shadowy deeps,
a flutter, a crunch, then suddenly food.
the wail of boatswain pales then peaks,
frantically grabbing at vanishing shoes,
mannequins lacking their muscle and meat,
of battling past a panicking crew,
then quietly breathe. leviathan squeeze,

choking on mast-wood, and splintering beams,

the crow Bijou ceased to beseech.

exposed wires

the dashboard in your truck is ripped out,
exposing the wires.
of which I, dripping in seawater
and reeling from vomit,
cannot touch.
a moment in time passes,
a tail wagging to greet me,
a broccoli pizza,
and ninety bucks later, I'm finally home.

I hope we will find each other.

reindeer and warplanes

I gazed into the godless sky
that opened up and rattled down,
then stood upon its silhouette with antler's out.
a snout aloft to raining bombs
would cry aloud in cattle clouds,
and drown in hottish dairy blood
they wrung from "witness battle" cows.

it's fairly dud,
the shoving bits of fur and cud
into my gasping, hurried lungs
to detonate... or close enough.

to wrap the world in blurry mud.
to halve the herd to wormy guts.
to laugh into the urn to learn
that death, today, ain't turning up.

fringillidae

thank you for reminding me,
our experience is valid,
even if they aren't the same.
thank you for the time you spent,
providing colour to a memory,
and allowing me remission of my pain.

surviving

how do I write about our journey
without falling apart,
when every little motion pushes into our scars?
I'm more afraid than I've ever been
and I've been pretty fucking scared,
so give me a second.
I'm trying my best.

as a cat

I'd be sneaky and slow.

frequently checking the trail of cheese
that would lead to Rodentian nose.
or, at the very least, a castle and moat,
where a gate made aware of a wary approach
would defensibly close.

I'd wiggle my toes,
and chase rats through the dangers of fibreglass.
through the wires and trash,
and the strung-up fly gut byways
where spidermen pass.

also, I'd take naps.

this feels fleeting

can't really seem to stay focused.
a buzz in my brain like a locust.
this is bogus. I just want to write,
to heal the trauma I've let in my life.

unstuck

tendons tighten, wrapped around a cracked skin,
and motion to depression that was tracked in.
I take one,
and another day's past in sadness,
so I fear that I can't win.
I take one,
and another day passes.
I'm still stuck in this habit.
I take one,
and another day's past.
here's to hoping that it lasts.

9 789357 447980